MEL BAY PRESENTS
Favorite Classics for Acoustic Guitar
BY BEN BOLT

Cover guitar by Pimentel & Sons

CD Contents

1. Funeral March of a Marionette [1:47]
2. Invention [1:41]
3. Liebestraum [1:50]
4. Greensleeves [:55]
5. The Old Castle [1:53]
6. Prelude No. 1 [1:37]
7. Clair de Lune [2:27]
8. Poetic Waltz [1:41]
9. Largo [2:14]
10. Andante [1:40]
11. Allegro [:17]
12. Dance [:47]
13. Galliard [:53]
14. Moderato [1:57]
15. Saltarello [:55]

Visit us on the Web at http://www.melbay.com — E-mail us at email@melbay.com

Contents

Songs marked with the * appear on the accompanying CD.

Author's Foreword

Nothing builds self-esteem for an artist more quickly than being invited to play an encore for an enthusiastic audience. Every acoustic guitarist remembers his or her first encore—it's a very special moment.

Unfortunately, the repertoire of the guitar has neglected the issue of what to play at the end of a performance. Consequently, the audience may listen to music that is unfamiliar or too long. The audience may also feel the artist is playing for self-enjoyment.

Keep in mind that the audience is responsible for your return to the stage. You can give back their appreciation and energy by selecting encores like "Claire de Lune," "Greensleeves," and "Liebestraum." These are familiar and well-loved pieces and will leave the audience with a pleasant feeling.

Relax and have fun when the audience brings you back with their cheers and applause!

Be seeing you.

Ben Bolt

About the Author

Ben Bolt is an excellent guitar player, with fine tone. —Andres Segovia

Ben Bolt was playing lead guitar in rock bands at age 12 and was performing professionally at age 16 in Miami night clubs.

After high school, Bolt left his band to study classical guitar in Spain. At age 19, he studied with Andres Segovia in Madrid. Segovia awarded Bolt a full scholarship to study at the international conservatory, Musica en Compostela.

After graduating from Musica en Compostela, Bolt studied with Abel Carlevaro in Paris. Carlevaro invited him to attend the 1974 International Guitar Seminary in Brazil under full scholarship.

In 1975, Bolt competed with students from 13 countries and won the coveted Merit Prize as Outstanding Student at the First International Masters Class in Montevideo, Uruguay.

Bolt also studied under the direction of Guido Santorsola, the Distinguished Italian composer, at the international music conservatory in Montevideo. After graduating with highest honors, Bolt went on concert tours throughout Central and South America.

At his concert debut in Uruguay, critics proclaimed him to be "a true maestro." A Panama reviewer stated . . . "He has a rapport with the composer that spells the difference between mere technical ability and virtuosity."

Bolt is an endorsee of Takamine guitars, Trace acoustic amps, and D'Addario strings. He has been featured in Mike Varney's Spotlight column in *Guitar Player*. His classical guitar arrangements have appeared in *Guitar* magazine.

Bolt records for Rosemary Records. He is the author of several best-selling books published by Mel Bay Publications.

He resides in Knoxville, Tennessee, where he teaches all styles of guitar. He is also Professor of Guitar at Carson-Newman College in Jefferson City, Tennessee.

Tablature
(Tab)

Tablature is an ancient way to write music. It is still used today because it is so easy to learn.

Tab is written on six lines. These six lines represent the six strings of the guitar. See example.

Strings: 1st
        2nd
        3rd
        4th
        5th
        6th

Numbers represent the spaces or frets to be played. This example means to play 1st, 3rd, and 5th frets in order of left to right, like reading words:

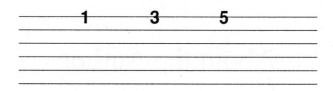

If the numbers are written in a vertical line, it means to play these numbers *simultaneously*.

E Chord

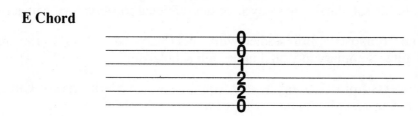

Music

Pitch

Music is written on five lines. These lines are called the **staff.** The notes can be written on the lines or in the spaces between the lines.

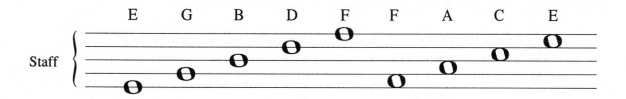

Notes above or below the staff require additional lines as a continuation of the staff. These lines are called **ledger lines.**

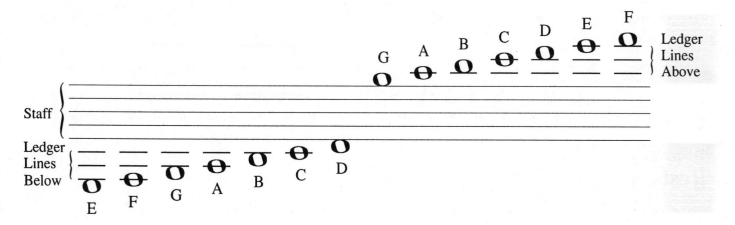

The musical alphabet uses the first seven letters of the language alphabet: A, B, C, D, E, F, G. After G, the next letter is A again. From any letter to the same letter is called an **octave.** There are eight letters in an octave.

One Octave: C D E F G A B C

At the beginning of every staff, you will notice a sign called the **clef sign.** In guitar music, we use the G or treble clef sign.

Clef Sign

Sharps, Flats, and Naturals

Sharp, flats, and naturals raise or lower a note by 1 fret. A 1-fret distance on the guitar is called a **half step** in music (or **half tone**). Each sharp, flat, and natural has a sign that is placed before the note.

Sharp ♯ raises the note by 1 fret.

Flat ♭ lowers the note by 1 fret.

Natural ♮ restores the note to its regular pitch after it was raised or lowered.

The way a note is written determines the length of the note's duration.

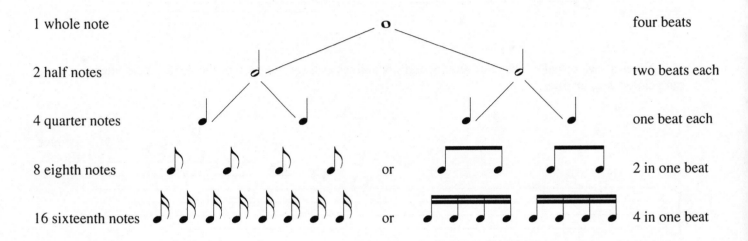

1 whole note		four beats
2 half notes		two beats each
4 quarter notes		one beat each
8 eighth notes	or	2 in one beat
16 sixteenth notes	or	4 in one beat

Rests

For every note value, there is a corresponding rest having the same time value.

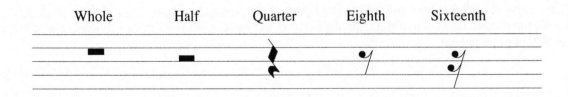

Music is arithmetically divided into **measures** by vertical bars in the staff. The number of beats in each measure is determined by the time signature placed after the clef:

$$\frac{2}{4} \qquad \frac{3}{4} \qquad \frac{4}{4} \qquad \frac{3}{8} \qquad \frac{6}{8} \quad \text{etc.}$$

The top number tells how many beats in a measure, while the bottom number tells what kind of note receives one beat.

$$\begin{aligned} \mathbf{3} \\ \mathbf{4} \end{aligned} \begin{aligned} = \\ = \end{aligned} \begin{aligned} \text{three beats to the measure} \\ \text{1 quarter note per beat} \end{aligned}$$

$\begin{matrix} \mathbf{3} & = & \text{three beats to the measure} \\ \mathbf{4} & = & \text{1 quarter note per beat} \end{matrix}$
or the equivalent:
2 eighth notes per beat
or 4 sixteenth notes per beat, etc.

The most common time signature is $\frac{4}{4}$. It is also marked **C** .

Key Signature

When the tonality requires that certain notes are to be sharp or flat throughout a composition, the sharps or flats are grouped together at the beginning of each staff, forming the **key signature.** This affects every note of the same name throughout the musical piece.

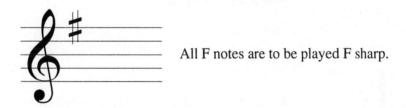

All F notes are to be played F sharp.

The Dot

A dot placed to the right of a note lengthens it by one half:

These dots can also be placed to the right of rests:

The Double Sharp

A double sharp placed before a note raises it by 2 frets, or a whole tone. G double sharp will sound like A. The sign looks like this:

✗

The Double Flat

The double flat lowers a note 2 frets, or a whole tone. E double flat will sound like D. The sign uses two flats before a note:

Repeats

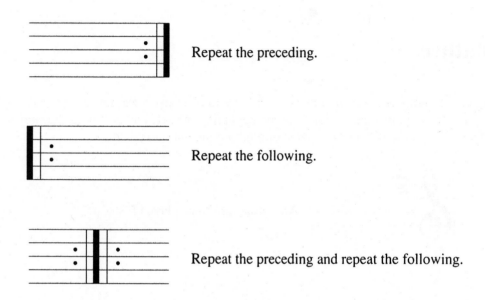

Repeat the preceding.

Repeat the following.

Repeat the preceding and repeat the following.

The Right Hand

Fingering

English		Symbol		Spanish
Thumb	=	*p*	=	Pulgar
Index	=	*i*	=	Indice
Middle	=	*m*	=	Medio
Ring	=	*a*	=	Anular

Position

The best way to learn a good right-hand position is to place *i, m,* and *a* on the third string. Place your thumb on the third string as well, keeping the thumb to the left of the index finger. (See sketch.)

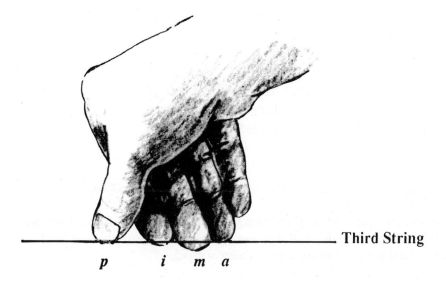

————————————————————————— Third String

p   *i*   *m* *a*

Strokes

The rest stroke using the thumb: Place *a* on the first string, *m* on the second string, and *i* on the third string. Play the sixth string slowly. As you glide over the string, follow through until you reach the fifth string. You should end up resting on string number 5. Practice on all bass strings (6, 5, and 4).

The rest stroke using the fingers: Place the thumb *(p)* on the sixth string. Play the third string slowly with your index *(i)* finger. As your finger glides slowly over the string, follow through until you rest on string number 4. Practice using your middle finger *(m)* on the second string and your ring finger *(a)* on the first string. Also, practice alternating *im, ia,* and *ma* on the treble strings (1, 2, and 3). I use *i* and *a* because they are similar in length on my hand. You should collapse the joint closest to the tip of the finger during the follow-through.

Free stroke: In using free stroke, the finger does not rest. The joint closest to the tip of the finger does not collapse. You must be careful **not** to get under the string and pull up will the finger. As an experiment, you can try pulling the string straight up and releasing it. This will cause a slap against the fingerboard and should be avoided. However, rock bass players use this technique as an effect that sounds good!

Regardless of which stroke is used, the flesh and fingernail should touch the string at the same time when you're preparing to play. This technique produces the best tone.

The Left Hand

Fingering

Index	=	1
Middle	=	2
Ring	=	3
Little Finger	=	4

Position

Because music changes pitch and direction, the left hand also needs to follow that motion. This makes explaining the left-hand position difficult, because it depends on your technical needs at that time. However, there are some practical and general concepts to keep in mind.

First, the fingernails of the left hand should be short enough so that they do not touch the fingerboard of the guitar. Second, the thumb should be placed generally in the middle of the back of the neck between the index and middle fingers. (See sketch.)

Third, the fingers should always be placed directly behind the frets. This gives the best tone and helps to teach your arm and finger exactly where each note is. Correct muscular memory begins here. Last, when playing scale passages, the knuckles should be parallel to the fingerboard.

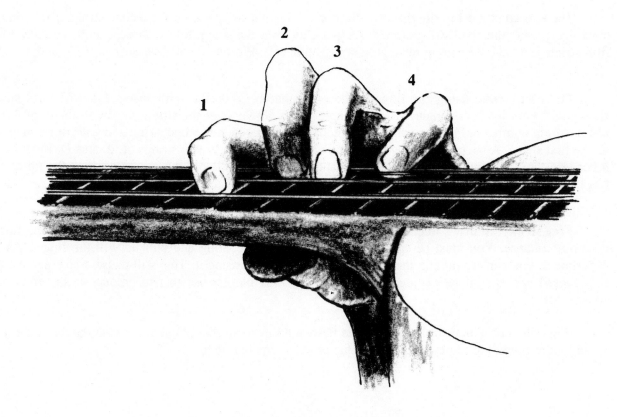

Funeral March of a Marionette

Arr. Ben Bolt

Charles Gounod

11

Invention

Arr. Ben Bolt

J.S. Bach

14

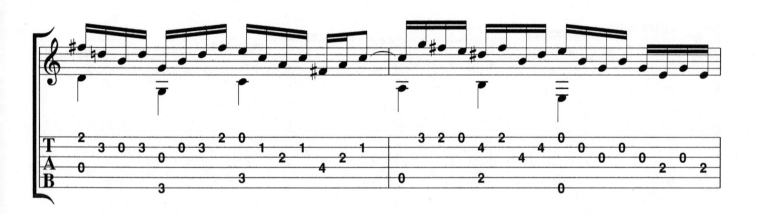

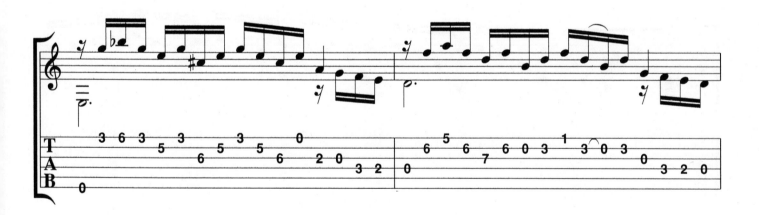

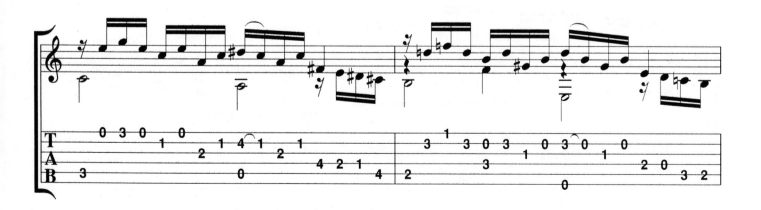

16

Liebestraum
(Dream of Love)

Arr. Ben Bolt

Franz Liszt

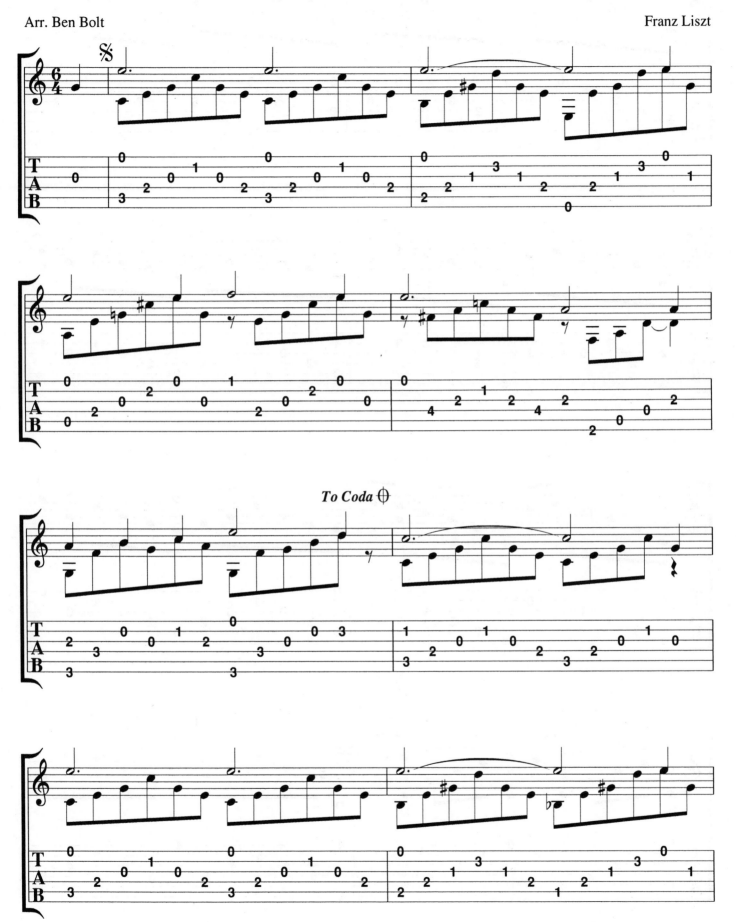

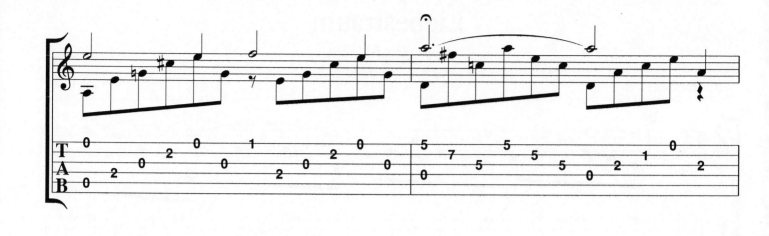

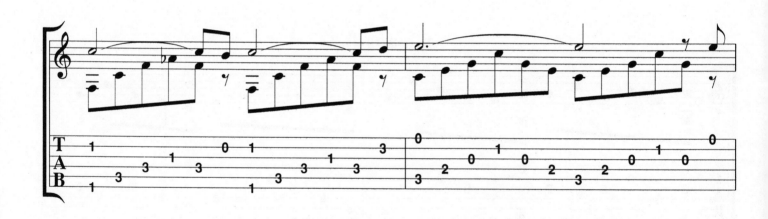

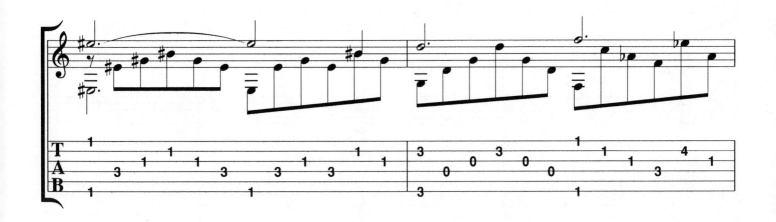

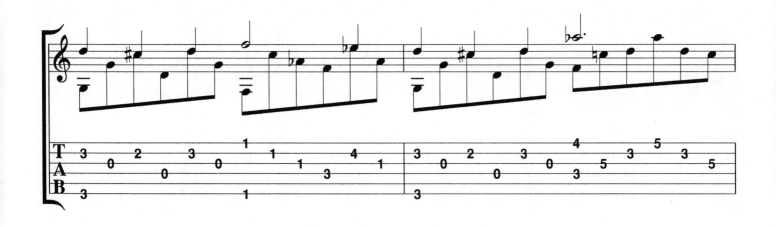

D.S. % al Coda ⊕   ⊕ Coda

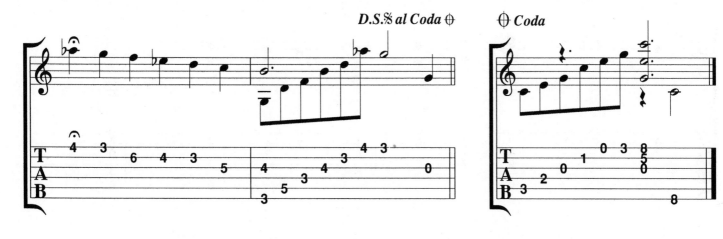

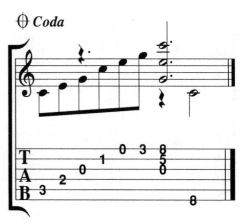

Greensleeves

Arr. Ben Bolt

Anon.

The Old Castle

Arr. Ben Bolt

Modest Mussorgsky

5th = G

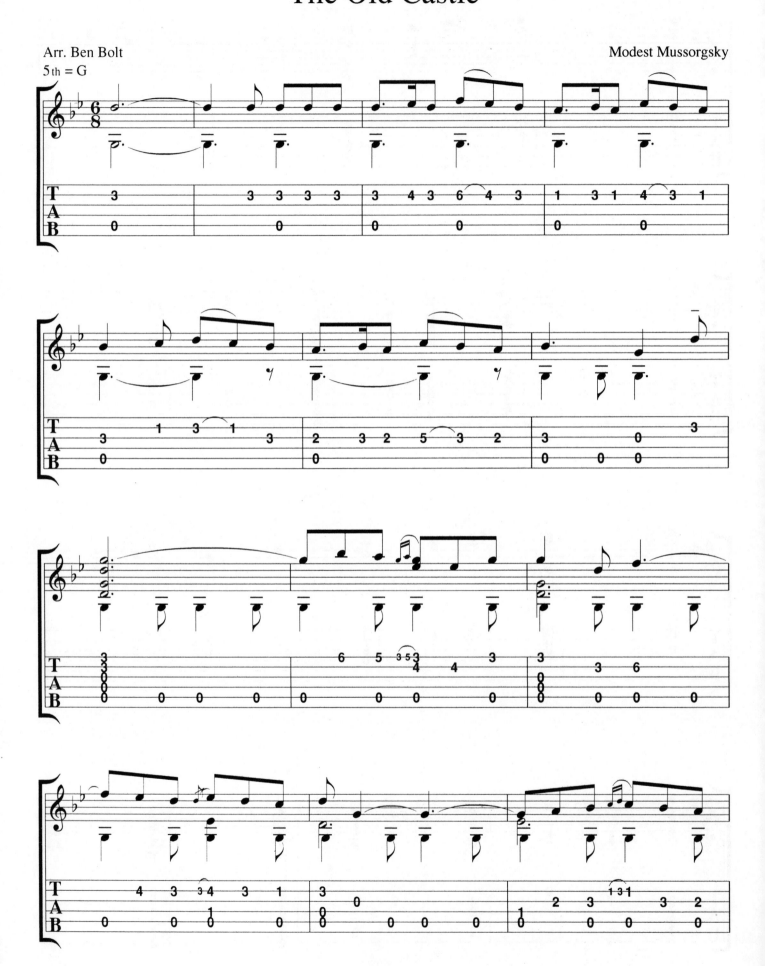

22

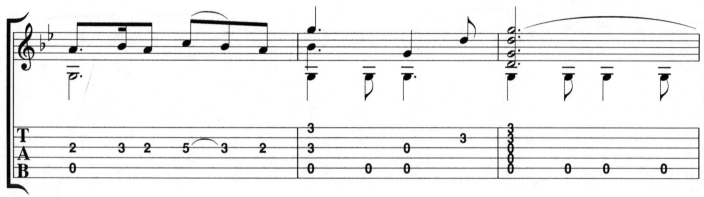

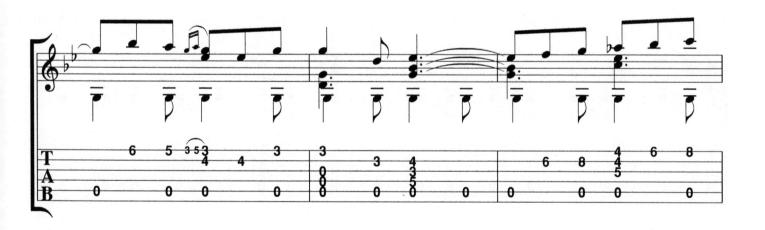

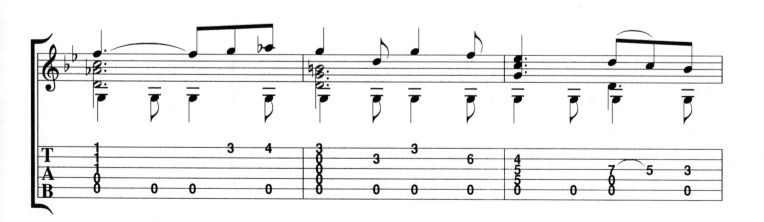

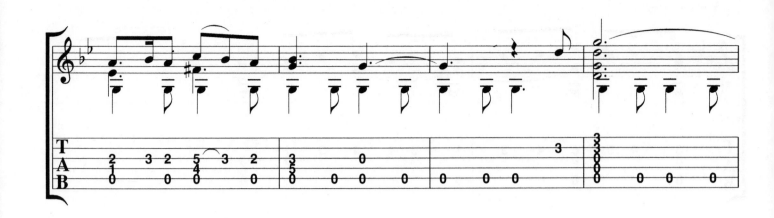

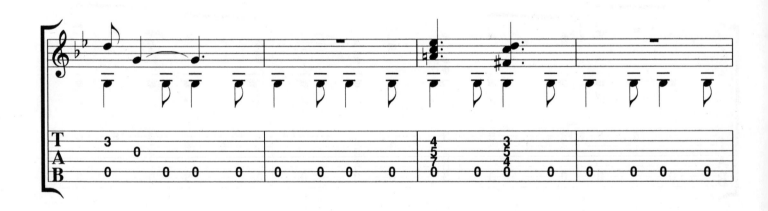

24

Prelude No. 1

Arr. Ben Bolt

J.S. Bach

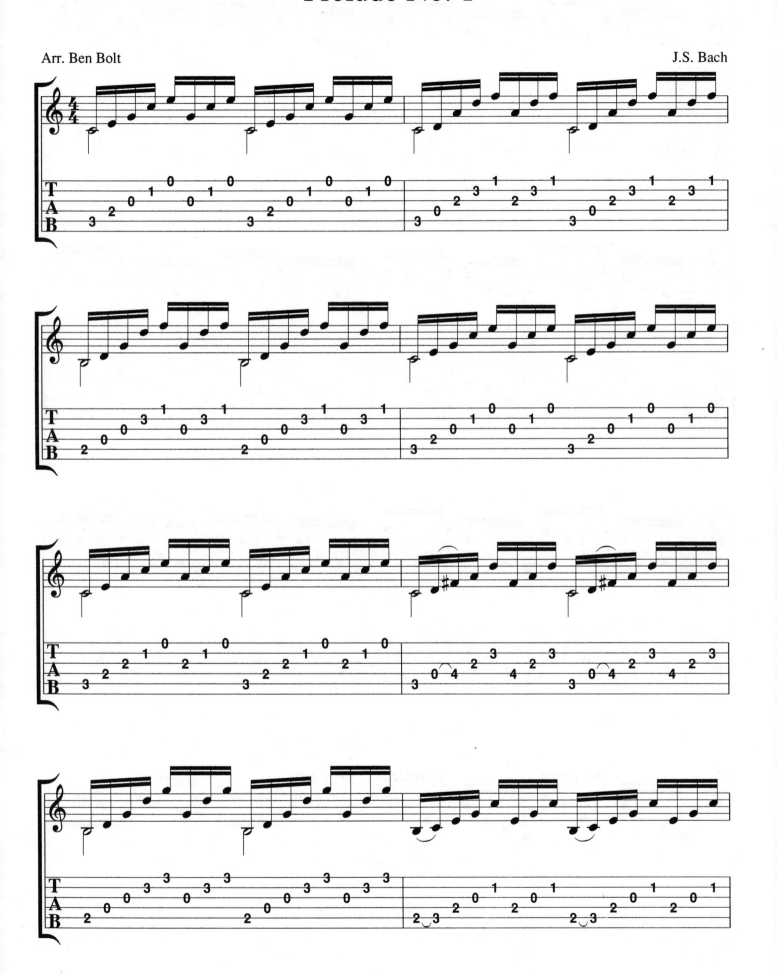

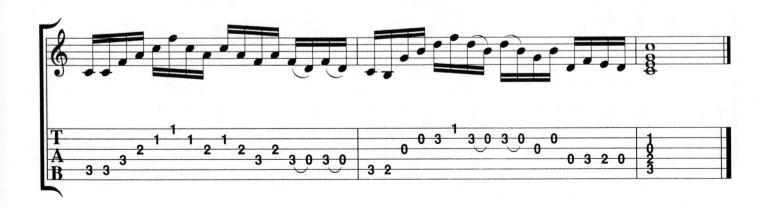

Clair De Lune

Arr. Ben Bolt
6th = D

Claude Debussy

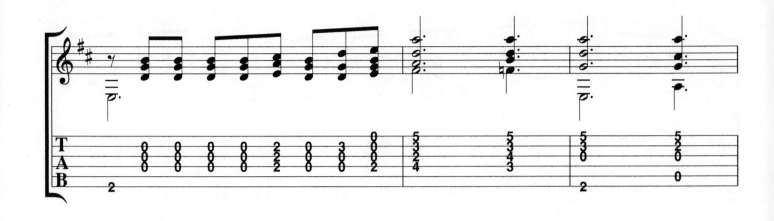

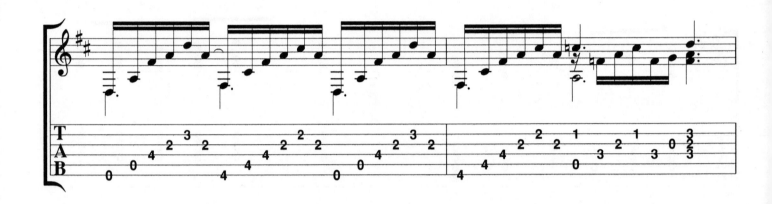

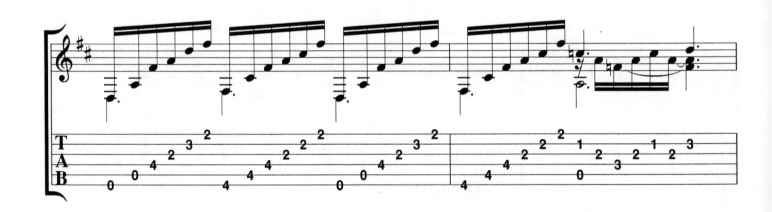

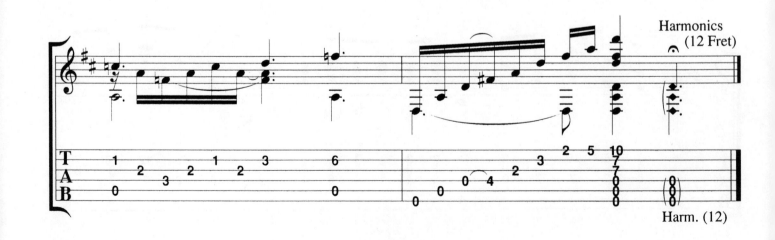

Poetic Waltz

Arr. Ben Bolt

Granados

Largo

Arr. Ben Bolt

Antonio Vivaldi

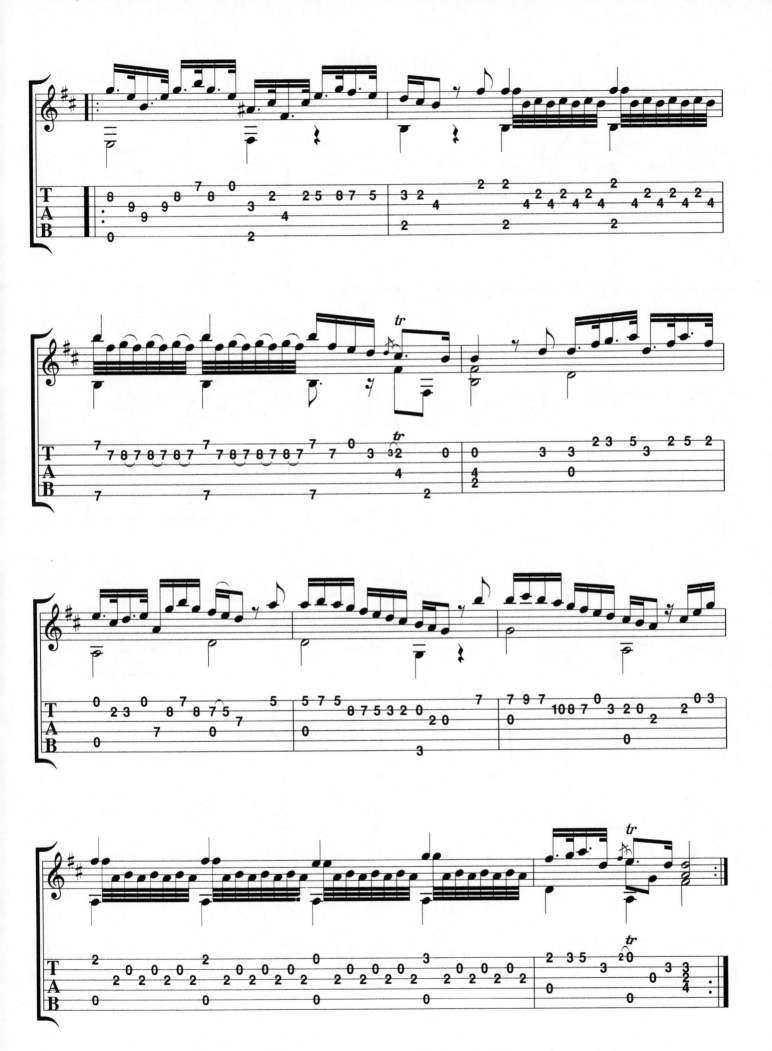

Andante

Arr. Ben Bolt

Anon.

Allegro

Arr. Ben Bolt

Anon.

37

Dance

Arr. Ben Bolt

Anon.

6th = D

This page has
been left blank to
avoid awkward
page turns

Galliard

Arr. Ben Bolt

Anon.

Moderato

Arr. Ben Bolt

Anon.

Saltarello

Arr. Ben Bolt

V. Galileo

6 th = D

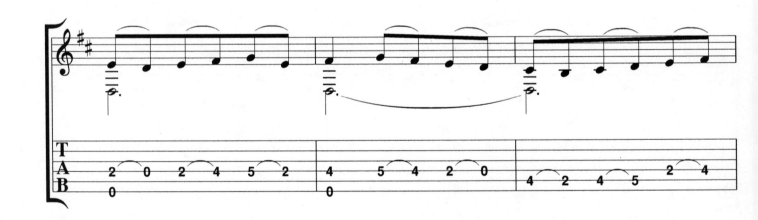

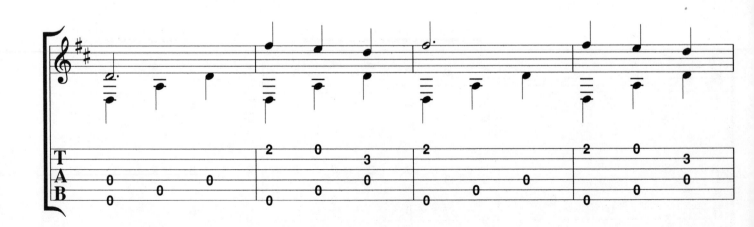

47

Other Titles
by Ben Bolt

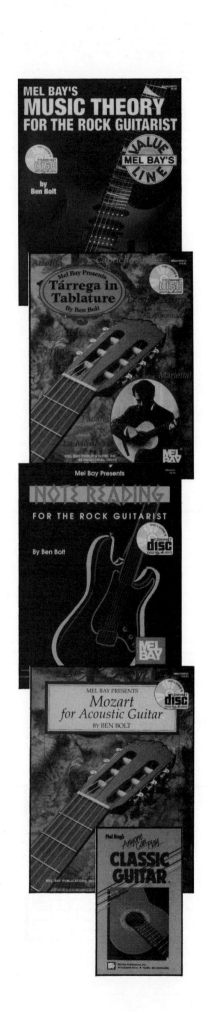

Music Theory for the Rock Guitarist by Ben Bolt. (94525BCD) Written in notation and tablature, this fine text presents basic information on building and playing blues scales, octaves, pentatonic scales, double stops, passing notes, modes, diatonic and chromatic scales, and chords and arpeggios. The rock guitarist is shown the principles of chord and scale formation, as well as how to use various aspects of theory and harmony correctly in performance. Book/CD set.

Tárrega in Tablature by Ben Bolt. (95689BCD) WIth his original compositions and transcriptions, Francisco Tárrega brought the classical guitar to new heights by giving it a repertoire of its own and influenced virtually every modern day classical guitarist. In this volume, Ben Bolt presents 29 pieces by Tárrega in standard notation and tablature. Titles include: "Lágrima," "Prelude in G," "Danza Mora," "Marieta!" (Mazurca), and many more. Text in English, Spanish, French, and Japanese. Written in standard notation and tab. Book/CD set.

Note Reading for the Rock Guitarist by Ben Bolt. (94813) Note reading is the key that can unlock the vast and exciting world of music. This unique and innovative system approaches it horizontally! Thus, instead of the usual manner of learning the natural notes in the first position, starting with the first string and going to the sixth, this method teaches all the natural notes on each string from left to right. In the author's words, "If you have tried to read music before and found yourself bored and frustrated, this book will give you hope." In notation and tablature. Book, cassette.

Mozart for Acoustic Guitar by Ben Bolt. (95526BCD) Because Mozart was a profoundly versatile composer, his music suits the guitar as well as it does a chamber orchestra. Playing this music on the guitar will impress your audience and provide a glimpse of Mozart's genius. Text is written in English, Spanish, French, and Japanese. In standard notation and tablature. Book/CD set.

Anyone Can Play Classic Guitar Video taught by Ben Bolt. (95082VX) In this video, you will learn from one of America's foremost classic guitar teachers. Ben Bolt demonstrates his principles for judging distance, point of reference, right- and left-hand positions, and the correct sitting posture. An easy-to-understand and technically correct introduction to classic guitar performance. 45-minute video.